TABLE OF CONTENTS

1 WHY I WROTE THIS BOOK

Many years ago, I found myself looking for a job. A good friend took me under his tutelage and gave me some excellent coaching on how to use my résumé effectively when interviewing for a job. I did what he said and immediately got a job earning twice what I was getting from my current employer. I never forgot what he taught me.

Not so many years ago, I was working for a company that got bought. In spite of the stellar performance of my team and me, suddenly I found myself holding a pink slip. My team was redundant.

I noticed that lots of my coworkers struggled with getting a new job, while I secured one very quickly - with the very company that had bought us out. And this wasn't the first time that had happened to me.

I decided to share what I know with others so that they can find it easier to quickly get to the job they want instead of facing the disappointment of job interviews that don't produce job offers.

This book is one in a series that will help you to Get and Keep the Job You Want.

These books teach you how to conduct an effective job search that finds lots of jobs that you can qualify for. How to write cover letters that get people to read your résumé. How to get a résumé that gets you interviews. And this volume, that teaches you how to interview so that you get the job offer.

2 WHY YOU SHOULD READ THIS BOOK

There are lots of job applicants out there chasing a limited number of positions. You need an edge.

Being unemployed is not fun. It tears at you deep inside and makes you question your worth.

Anything you can do to shorten the time you spend between jobs is going to directly improve your finances and your self-image.

Many job applicants make it all the way to the interview and then never get the job offer - wasting their time and leading to disappointment and discouragement. You don't have to be one of them.

I and my clients have used these same techniques again and again to walk out of interviews with job offers. Sometimes, I turned down the job, but I couldn't turn down a job that hadn't been offered. And, I have to tell you, it feels a whole lot better to be in control of the situation and be able to compare competing job offers and turn some down so that you can take the job you really want.

This book will help you to handle your interview effectively so that you can make the best impression and get a job offer while others just get an interview.

So, don't just take my word for it. Read this book and then get a couple of other books on interviewing so that you can be positive you are getting the best advice money can buy.

3 CONGRATULATIONS

Congratulations. You got the job interview.

Your résumé and cover letter did their jobs.

The cover letter got them to read your résumé, and your résumé convinced them to give you an interview.

Now, it is all up to you. If you nail the interview, they will probably make you an offer.

Interviewing well isn't rocket science, but it isn't a walk in the park either. It pays to keep some things in mind, and to follow a few simple ground rules.

In my career, I have read thousands of résumés and interviewed hundreds of job seekers. In addition to this on-the-job experience, I have been a Certified Professional Résumé Writer and run a business helping job seekers for many years. So I have seen résumés from both sides of the table.

Add to that, I have received some of the best training available in behavioral interviewing which helps people tasked with making hiring decisions to use highly focused questions to uncover the job seeker's relevant experience.

What follows in this book is advice distilled from my training and experience that will help you nail your interview, every time.

As you shift from blog posts to the materialsexclusive to this book, you will see some themes repeated. Pay attention.There is a test at the end of this. The test will be your next job interview, andwhether you get "A" job offer or "F"ail to get an offer depends on your
ability to learn and practice a few simple principles and techniques.

Let's start off with some real life examples pulled from one of my blog posts.

4 FIVE WAYS TO BLOW AN INTERVIEW
and Two Ways to Nail It.

Recently, I have found myself back on the hiring side of the job seeker table. This has given me a fresh opportunity to observe first-hand mistakes that job seekers make with their resumes and during their interview process.

While my recent experience has revolved around interviewing Senior Project Managers, people who specialize in managing multi-million dollar projects that have enterprise-wide impacts, the mistakes I have seen made by some of these job seekers (mostly experienced consultants) are surprisingly rookie errors. Errors that any could make. Errors that everyone can avoid.

In each case, these errors eliminated the candidate from further consideration for the role.

To be clear, each of these candidates was only the subject of a phone interview. Unfortunately, the phone interview was used to decide which of them would be invited to participate in a video interview, or a face-to-face. So, some of these errors are specific to phone interviews.

Error #1 - Focus on the interview.

One candidate blew his chances by clearly not being focused on the interview. From the background noise it was clear the candidate was in the car. That in itself isn't a killer. But, it seemed he got in and out of the vehicle, creating distracting noises. What is worse is that he may have muted the line temporarily to order his lunch at a fast food restaurant.

We didn't hear the lunch order, but we could clearly hear all the background noise that sounded like a fast food restaurant.

It was clear to all of us on the other end of the line, that Mr. Fast Food was putting an higher priority on getting his lunch rather than getting this job. Considering that the role comes with a six-figure annual pay, that seems a bit short-sighted.

If you are doing a phone interview, get to someplace quiet.

If you are in your car, find a place to pull over and give the interview your full attention, while keeping the background noise minimized.

Show the hiring team (or manager) that you value their time and the potential role enough to give it your full attention. Even if that means missing your lunch.

Error #2 - Failure to answer the question.

This one was made by Mr. Fast Food as well. When I asked him a question about dealing with difficult or demanding people, he described a standard change control process. When I asked the same question a different way, I got the same answer.

Really?!

I confess I have never considered using a change control process as a means to deal with relationship management issues. Maybe the next time my wife says we need to do something different, I will have her document her request, and then I will advise her of the pros and cons as well as the cost and schedule implications of her request. I'm sure that Mr. Fast Food actually does this in his life, right?

Focus on the question that is asked.

If you don't understand the question, ask a clarifying question to be sure you are on the right track. Then give your answer.

If you get two versions of the same question, chances are that you didn't answer it the first time. So, you need to use one or more clarifying questions to be sure you understand what your interviewer is truly asking.

Error #3 - Asking Irrelevant Questions.

The role we have been interviewing for is for a Project Manager to help gather business requirements. When the candidate asked about the technical architecture of the target system, it was a red flag that he was focused on the technology side, not the business side of the situation. His failure to understand where the role was aligned, knocked him out of the running with just one irrelevant question.

Ask questions to understand the role, to understand the organization, to understand why they are filling this position now.

Don't ask questions about things that are irrelevant to the role.

Error #4 - Using Team-Speak.

I had to stop several candidates in mid-answer because of this error.

We are so indoctrinated in corporate America *against* tooting our own individual horns that we often talk about what "we" do at work.

As I have pointed out in several of my books, when you are interviewing, the prospective employer is hiring you, not "we".

So, when the prospective employer asks, "what did you do?" Make sure your answer is appropriately focused on what "I" did.

As an experienced manager, I can tell you than when I keep getting "we" responses after trying to focus a candidate on the "I", my conclusion is that the candidate didn't actually do anything and is trying to take credit for the work of others by association. At that point, no matter how much longer the clock runs, the interview is done and you are not going to get the job.

Give credit to teammates where it is due. And make sure, when interviewing, that you claim the credit that is your due.

Error #5 - Resume Problems.

One candidate was hindered because the résumé we received omitted any references to any experiences since 2010. After the interview was over, the "head hunter" provided an updated résumé, but it was too late by then. You only get one chance to make a first impression and this guy's résumé made a bad one.

Make sure your résumé is up to date. And, make sure your prospective employer has your most current resume. Don't assume someone else handled it correctly for you. Get it right, in advance.

Two Ways to Nail It!

The Right Stuff #1 - Resume-based Responses.

One of the most impressive candidates got the green light for the next round because of what she did right in the interview. Her answers referred to specific experiences in her résumé. She noted the project and the employer, described the situation that related to the question, and then told us clearly what she did and how it worked out.

The Right Stuff #2 - Cold Hard Numbers.

Yes, size actually does matter.

When I am considering a project manager, I need to understand the breadth and depth of their experience. Key indicators I use are the number of people on their project team and the size of the project budget.

Because of my experience, I know that project managers whose biggest budget has been $1 million or less are in a different category than those who have led projects with budgets in the $10 million to $200 million range. And those whose projects have never exceeded $500k are in another (lower) category.

When I am looking to bring on a PM to run a project, or even a piece of a project, that has a $10 million or more budget, I would be irresponsible to make an offer to someone who has never played above the million dollar line before. And I would likely not be doing them, or me, any favors. That project manager would likely be in way over his or her head and would likely go down in flames. And could take down the project (and me) with them.

The cold hard numbers in the candidate's experience give me the warm-fuzzy feelings I need to move ahead when considering whether or not to make an offer, or move things to the next stage and bring them in for a face-to-face.

This fact of cold hard numbers is true in almost any role, from flipping burgers to selling products, to managing clients.

Consider two burger-flipping candidates:

#1 says she had worked for several different restaurants as a fry cook.

 #2 says she has worked for several different restaurants as a fry cook. Her résumé notes that she handled up to 20 orders per hour at peak times and typically earned a 99% accuracy rating from her employer, having less than 1% returns on orders.

In the interview, when you press #1 for numbers, her first response is "I don't know." When you push for estimates, you find out that she was comfortable handling up to 20 orders per hour, 40 at peak. When you ask about returns, you get a "1%" answer.

Which do you want to hire to work in your restaurant?

Now, look at yourself.

Consider the numbers that reflect the quantity and quality of the work you do. Identify them. Track your performance. And make sure you bring out those numbers when the time is right in your next job interview.

Get those cold, hard numbers to work for you and create a warm feeling in your bank account.

5 THE RIGHT APPROACH

Your purpose in an interview is to get the offer.

Unfortunately, too many people forget this.

Don't go into the interview with the purpose of determining whether or not you want that position. Instead, focus on doing what you should to get the offer.

A wise old career counselor once told me, "You cannot turn down an offer that hasn't been made." In other words, don't decide whether or not you want to work for someone until they have actually made you a job offer. Deciding before you have an offer is a lot like deciding whether to accept a marriage proposal when no one has asked you. It may give you a warm sense of satisfaction and control, but it is still just a fantasy playing out on the stage of your mind.

How do you get a job offer?

The answer to that question is simple. But, don't let the simplicity fool you.
It is not easy.

You get a job offer by communicating positive, relevant information about
yourself to the interviewer concisely in a believable manner.

To do this you need to control the interview and present yourself in a manner
that is consistent with the professional portrayed in your cover letter and
résumé.

Controlling the Interview

If you ponder for a moment what happens in an interview it become obvious
that the person asking the questions is controlling the interview.

One person asks a question and the other person responds. This is followed
by another question and another response, and so on. _Interviews are
controlled by asking appropriate questions._

You want to give the interviewer the information _you_ want them to have,
without allowing them to get into those areas where you are weak or which
might cause controversy. This must be done without the interviewer being
conscious that you have accomplished exactly what _they_ set out to do
themselves.

Your goal is not to totally control the interview, but it is necessary to be able
to take control when it is to your advantage, and to guide the conversation to
where you want it to focus.

At the end of the interview, the interviewer should feel that they have learned
what they wanted to know about you. They should not feel that they were
manipulated and forced to deal with you strictly on your terms. You do not
have to be a psychologist (or a hypnotist) to achieve this, you just need to use
The Nine Essential Strategies of Interviewing.

6 THE NINE ESSENTIAL STRATEGIES OF INTERVIEWING

What you need to know no matter what job you are interviewing for!

1. _Respond to all interviewer questions with the appropriate strategy or
answer._

Keep reading. This will explain itself as you study the remaining strategies.

2. Never volunteer information beyond what is asked for.

When you start to ramble or go beyond what the interviewer asked, you run the risk of saying things which may disqualify you for the job, or which may allow the interviewer to discriminate against you.

For example, if you are asked why you want the job, stick to the relevant facts regarding the opportunity, the company, your skills, and the job fit. Don't go on about how your wife/husband/mother/father/significant other/the voices in your head thought your last job was a dead end, or that your minister told you that you were destined for greatness.

3. After you have answered a question adequately, respond with a suitable question to verify if you are on the right track.

This will give the interviewer a chance to put you back on track if you misunderstood the question and will demonstrate an important communication skill – using feedback.

4. If you are not sure what the interviewer wants, ask them to clarify the question.

It is a sign of a good communicator that you don't make assumptions.

Asking clarifying questions lets the interviewer know that you don't run off half-cocked, that you make sure you understand the question before responding.

After you ask, listen closely to the answer. Often their response will give you the best answer to the question.

5. Answer open-ended questions only after attempting to get clarification from the interviewer as to what they want.

This narrows the scope of the question and gives you the opportunity to pick up information about what they are looking for (see #4 above).

6. When you don't want to answer the question as stated, or are unsure about how to answer without causing problems, ask for clarification.

In responding, the interviewer will often give you the out you need or additional information which helps you answer the question properly.

This is a lot like #4 also, but the difference here is that the interviewer has asked you something which makes you uncomfortable.

Rather than choose between giving an answer you don't like and telling a lie (a definite No! No!), you respond with a question that redirects the conversation closer to where you want it to be.

7. Banish from your mind and conversation all negative expressions, words, phrases, thoughts, sentences, and answers throughout the interview, and during the before and after phases, too.

Don't mention that your last boss was a jerk.

Or that your coworkers were brainless idiots.

Or that the company president couldn't find his fanny with both hands.

Or that you have this little bad habit...well, you get the idea.

8. If the interviewer appears to have an objection to a specific issue, ask probing questions to uncover the root of the objection. Then, respond to the root of the objection.

This saves a lot of time and avoids volunteering too much information.

For example, the interviewer asks, "I see you used to work for our cross-town rival?" You respond, "Yes. Is that a problem?"

9. If there is an obvious issue which may lead the interviewer to reject you out of hand, bring it up yourself in a positive manner which reflects well on you, and which addresses the probable objection they will have.

Then use questions to determine what they are thinking so that you can pursue it further if necessary.

If you use these nine strategies, they will keep the interview close to your sweet spot where you can let your experience and abilities shine like a jewel. A jewel that they want on their team.

Now, please consider what you may not have thought about the parts of the interview and why this matters to you.

7 THE THREE VITAL PARTS OF AN INTERVIEW
What should you do before, during and after the interview?

There are three parts to the interview.

1. Pre-Interview
2. The Interview
3. Closing and Follow-up

The interview actually begins when you set the appointment, and continues when you arrive at the building. It isn't over until you have left the premises. Each part of the interview has clear landmarks and expectations you should meet.

If you fail to grasp this simple truth, you will blow your interview before you even knew it started.

1. Pre-interview

The Pre-interview begins when you set the appointment and lasts right up until the interviewer meets you and asks you his or her first question.

Preparing for the Appointment (bring this information with you to the interview)

1. The date and time of the interview.
2. The name of the interviewer or the person for whom to ask.
3. The exact location of the building, if it's in a complex, and where you need to go within it.
4. Specific directions to the building if the location is not familiar to you.
5. Get the job title and *all* other information about the position that your contact is willing to volunteer before the interview.
6. Arrive ten minutes early.
7. If you are going to be late or unavailable for the interview, immediately call and notify the company of your circumstances. Attempt to reset your appointment.
8. Bring extra copies of your résumé printed on premium quality paper.
9. Always do your homework! Get any information you can about recent company performance, structure, officers, and

products.

Dressing for the Interview

1. Do not dress casually, regardless of the dress code where you are interviewing. It is almost always better to dress a little more formally than required, rather than being too casual.

2. Darker colors and conservative styles tend to be most appropriate for interviewing.

3. Be certain your choice of colors and style is appropriate. When in doubt, find out what the supervisors who will be interviewing you wear, and copy them.

4. Unless you are interviewing for a job as an exotic dancer, never wear suggestive or sexually provocative clothing to an interview. Your choice of clothes and styles should demonstrate to the employer that you take the position seriously.

5. For men, a two or three-piece suit is appropriate.

6. For women, a skirted suit or pant suit with close-toed shoes is appropriate for most situations.

(Further guidelines can be found in _Dress for Success_ by John T. Molloy or How to Dress for Success by Edith Head)

In the Waiting Room

1. Keep calm. Don't act nervous. Take deep breaths and let them out slowly to calm yourself.

2. While waiting, prepare for the interview in your mind and how you will handle different aspects of it. Don't bring any kind of worksheet with you.

3. Ask to look at company literature if it is not already on display. Read it and use any relevant information in the interview. Don't read irrelevant materials (e.g., novels, comic books, fashion magazines, etc.) as they will distract you from focusing on the interview.

4. Do not be overly friendly or chatty with others in the waiting area or with the receptionist.

5. *Never* flirt with anyone during the interview process.

2. The Interview

The Introduction

Shake hands with each person interviewing you. Look each one in the eye and state your name. Address the interviewer **by name** and mention the title of the position you are interviewing for.

Note: This is an extremely important step, which needs to be followed. It can tip the scales very dramatically in your favor right at the beginning of the interview. Interview success or failure is often determined at, or near, the beginning of the interview.

The Discussion

Experience: First, provide specific, appropriate experiences relating to the position. Then, mention experiences that relate in a more general manner, as appropriate.

Education: Mention those aspects that specifically relate to the position first, then mention those which relate more generally to the position, as needed.

Personal Assets: First, bring up those characteristics that relate specifically to the needs of the position, and then move on to those of a more general nature, as needed.

These factors should be brought up in the order of their relevance to the position you are seeking.

Regardless of whether or not your résumé has preceded you, never assume that the interviewer has read it. Or if they have, that they understand the connections between the position and your experience.

Always explain what you say in such a way that draws attention to the relevant information in your résumé, and describe how it applies to the job.

<u>Applicant Questions</u>: It is very important to have prepared relevant questions which demonstrate an interest in the position and a knowledge of the company.

There are many non-controversial questions which could be raised.

Ask questions which reflect a knowledge of company operations and of the position. This is where your homework pays off.

3. Closing and Follow-up

Tell the interviewer that you enjoyed the interview and are definitely interested in the position, even if you don't think you are at the moment, because you may regret closing that door later on.

Send a letter to each person who interviewed you, thanking them for their time, and again expressing your interest in the position (see Part II: Tips for Effective Cover Letters for tips applicable to this letter).

Often, the interviewer won't tell you when the final decision on the position is being made. The following approach is very helpful:

Ask directly when they will be making a decision.

> Then say, "So, you'll be making the decision by _____?
> Great! I'll call you on _____. Would the morning or
> afternoon be better for you?"

Notice that you do not give the interviewer the choice of whether or not you will call.

If you get the message that you have been rejected, ask for leads to other positions which might be suitable for you. This is best done by using a magical phrase that works well in many circumstances, "Who do you know who…"

For example:

"Who do you know who might be hiring someone with my qualifications?"

This question has the benefit of getting results without putting undue pressure on the person you are asking.

Also note the difference between asking, "Who do you know…" versus "Do you know anyone who…" When you ask, "Do you know…" you will get a simple "Yes" or "No", and you are all done. In contrast, when you ask, "Who do you know…", you might get a one brusque "No one," but, you are much more likely to get a thoughtful answer that includes names and contact information.

8 HANDLING COMMONLY ASKED INTERVIEW QUESTIONS

Some of the most commonly asked interview questions are, "What is your greatest strength?", "What is your greatest weakness?", and "Tell me about a time when you failed."

Many job seekers think these are trick questions, and they can be. But, if you handle them correctly they will become opportunities for you to showcase your abilities.

First, let's tackle the easiest one, "What are (or is) your greatest strength(s)."

Right away, make sure you <u>listen</u> to the question. If some asks you about your greatest strength, singular. Absolutely do not list more than one strength.

A recent job seeker made that mistake. My colleague asked, "Tell me, what is your single greatest strength?"

The candidate replied confidently, "Communication." Then, after a brief pause, added "and my attention to detail and ability to persevere and get things done."

Job lost.

Why?

Because this self-described great communicator didn't know how to listen. My colleague's question was clear. "What is your <u>single</u> greatest strength." He didn't ask for the top three or top two. He only asked for the top one.

By not listening and giving more than one strength, the job seeker showed that he was actually a very lousy communicator. And, if communication was his greatest strength, then the rest of that list was not going to be any better.

Here is how you can learn to answer that question truthfully, fully, and in a way that will deliver a powerful punch in your interview.

What is your greatest strength?

First, answer the question for yourself, outside of the interview. If you don't know the answer off the top of your head, then do the following exercise to figure out the answer.

Grab a pen or pencil and in the space below list three times when you were totally absorbed in what you were doing and lost track of time.

#1 - I totally lost track of time when I was…

#2 - Another time I got absorbed in what I was doing and totally lost track of time was when I …

#3 - A third time I recall that I got so absorbed in what I was doing that I totally lost track of time was when …

Now that you have noted three times when you were so engaged in what you were doing that you lost track of time you need to determine what skill you were exhibiting at the time.

Even if one of those was that you lost track of time fishing, or shopping, these are valid examples. When you lose track of time fishing, you may be exhibiting patience as a strength. When you lose track of time shopping, chances are you are looking at various alternatives, envisioning the outcomes, and making detailed comparisons. This attention to detail and the ability to compare alternatives and see the outcomes in your mind is you exhibiting a strength.

In any case, you need to sift through these three experiences and find the strengths that you are exhibiting.

Now that you have identified your top three strengths, you need to learn how to turn this information into a powerful one-two punch for your interview.

Allow me to repeat myself here.

The most powerful interviewing technique I have ever learned is called the STAR technique. It is immensely helpful as an interviewer. And, as a job seeker it is very powerful.

The "ST" in STAR is where you explain the situation you were in or the task(s) you were given.

The "A" is where you explain the "Activities" that you personally did to remedy the situation. Remember, "we-speak" is not your friend here. Make a clear distinction between any "we" activities and the "I did…" activities.

The "R" is all about the "Results" that came from how you handled the situation.

You can use the STAR technique to your advantage when answering this question by:

1. When asked about your greatest strength don't take time to think about it. Simply and promptly respond, "My greatest strength is…" and fill in what your strength is. Then,

2. Follow that statement with, "And, the reason I believe that is my

greatest strength is because…", and now you tell them about one of your experiences where you lost track of time and ended up with very satisfying results.

3. Relate your experience to the work they are wanting you to do and explain how your strength in this area has helped you in the past and how it may help solve whatever problem(s) they are facing that you are supposed to resolve.

4. Practice your answer outside the interview and make sure you can deliver your answer within two minutes. If your answer takes longer than five minutes, you absolutely, positively must refine your answer and be able to deliver it as close to two minutes as possible.

5. After you give your answer, ask, "Did that answer your question?"

When you can answer a question like this without hesitation and without wasting a bunch of time, while giving specific evidence and experiences where you exhibited this strength it makes a powerful impression on a prospective employer. It demonstrates a level of self knowledge and confidence that most interviewers don't see very often.

Remember this STAR technique, as well as the need to practice your answer(s) and your follow-up question, "Did that answer your question?" These same lessons should be used with every answer you give to an interview question.

Now, let's tackle the last two questions, each in turn.

What is your greatest weakness?

"What is your greatest weakness?" This question often strikes terror into the heart of job seekers. They see it as a trick question. And too often, they try to give a trick answer.

Giving a trick answer that is really a "humble brag" usually isn't the best course of action. Honesty is still the best policy.

To really figure out your greatest weakness, once again you will answer three questions:

#1 - I was most miserable when …

#2 - Another time I was most miserable was when I was doing ….

#3 - A third time I was very unhappy was when ….

If much of these three experiences revolve around the actions of others, that is not a bad answer.

Consider what the other people around you did that may have triggered your misery. Perhaps they let you down. Perhaps they asked you to do something you weren't good at. Perhaps, they tortured you in other ways.

Regardless, identify the themes and then you will likely have your answer.

I am going to give you an example from my own life. Perhaps this will help you to apply this to yourself.

I was hired as a project manager by a major national bank in the U.S. to build the automation infrastructure to support their operational risk management system. Which I did. Once it was built, they kept me around to run it for a time and work out the problems. Which I did, for a year. This new role is something called operations management.

Operations management has many similarities with project management and some very key differences. The skills needed for both roles are almost identical, but in a very different mix from one role to the other.

And, most importantly of all to me, the nature of the work was dramatically different.

Project managers build systems and processes. They ensure that the processes are working effectively, often within some pretty broad tolerances. To fix problems with the systems or processes, they may use some forceful approaches to move people from old habits into new ways of doing things.

Operations managers refine and improve existing systems and processes. Where the project manager was moving the dial from zero to 99%, the operations manager is likely to be trying to move the dial from 99% to 99.99%. This small, but important shift usually requires much more patience with people and a much more subtle touch than most project managers exhibit.

Where project managers periodically get to face new challenges with new projects, the operations manager faces the same challenges week in and week out, month in and month out, year in and year out.

After a year of acting as the operations manager, I sat down in my boss' office one morning and told him he needed to fire me and to hire a real operations manager. After he got over his initial shock, I told him why.

I explained to him that project management gets me up in the morning, while operations management keeps me up at night. I told him I was tired of staying up at night and not wanting to get up in the morning.

I consider operations management to be my greatest weakness. It is not because I cannot do it. I have done it successfully. Rather it is because it makes me miserable to do it.

If a prospective employer is thinking of hiring me into a job that is too much like an operations management role, I would rather keep looking than to live in misery. If I really needed the job and the offered it to me, I would do it with the clear understanding that it would only be for a year or so.

I handled 18 weeks of Marine Corps Boot Camp. I can handle being miserable in good-paying civilian work for a year.

Can you?

Either way, answer 'your greatest weakness question' honestly. It will likely save you from getting locked into a role where you live a life of quiet desperation.

And don't forget to put your answer into a STAR format. Practice your answer. Time your response to get it close to two minutes. And, follow up with, "Did that answer your question?"

What is your greatest failure?

Okay, on to question number three. "What is your greatest failure?"

Although you may think this is a trick question, it really isn't.

The fact is, no one wins all the time. If you claim you don't have any failures, then you are either lacking in experience, or lying through your teeth. Neither is a very good basis for getting a job offer.

To answer this question won't require you to answer three questions. You already know what you believe is your greatest failure.

What most employers want to learn from your answer to this is:

1. Are you honest enough to admit failure?

2. Are you experienced enough to have failed?

And here is the real meat of this matter…

3. Can you and have you learned from your failure?

4. Did you let failure define you, or did you rise above it?

So, the exercise for you to do now is to list only one or two of your biggest failures. Then under each, list the lessons you learned from each experience and what you would do differently if you were once again faced with a similar experience.

While you are thinking about that, let me share one more of my failures with you.

I was tasked by the Division President within a Fortune 500 company to run a major, high risk project. One of the key elements in the project was a team of sales people and their leaders. I dealt directly with their leadership.

These sales leaders had been recruited in from outside the company. They were fiercely independent, highly compensated and utterly confident that without their cooperation the effort would fail.

When I required one of these sales leaders to provide me with answers to certain key project questions, he took exception to me pressuring him for a timely response.

He invited me into a conference room and shut the door behind him.

Once in the room, he confronted me.

"Who the hell do you think you are requiring me to answer your questions?" He remained standing as he peeled off his jacket and tossed it onto the back of the chair I had thought he was going to sit in.

I looked up from my seat and calmly replied.

"I think I am the guy who the Division President tasked with getting these questions answered promptly and completely so that we can keep this effort moving the direction it needs to go."

At this point, he began to shout and pushed up his sleeves as though he was preparing to throw a punch.

"I am a senior vice president and a sales manager, and the last time I looked, I don't report to you."

I realized that he was between me and the door. I couldn't step past him to open the door and leave without risking him interpreting it as me moving toward him to fight.

I evaluated my options, believing that he might well throw a punch at me any second.

If I hit him first, I would definitely get fired.

If he hit me, well… I wasn't keen on letting that happen.

I determined that I would let him hit me once without punching back. But, if he went for a second swing, I would take him out.

I stood up and stepped a half-step closer to him and looked him straight in the eyes.

"I am the project manager on this effort and it is my job to make sure this effort succeeds." I answered.

He looked me in the eyes, we were about the same height, and I believe at that moment he realized a couple of things:

1. His bullying tactics that worked so well in the struggle between sales and back office types would not work with me. And,

2. He was standing toe to toe with a US Marine who could likely take him out and leave him in pain for a very long time.

He blinked.

Then, someone who had heard the shouting opened the door and asked if everything was all right.

I said, "Everything is fine. I was just leaving." I stepped past him and out of the office we were in.

What lesson did I learn from this?

Now, whenever I go into an enclosed space for a meeting with someone who I anticipate may be confrontational, I make sure that I am positioned so that I can de-escalate the situation by leaving without having to go closer to them to get out of the room.

Now, tell me about the top three on your hit parade of failures and what you learned from each.

#1 - the first failure that comes to mind is when…

What I learned from this is…

#2 - the second failure that I immediately recall is when….

From this experience I learned…

#3 - the third biggest failure I had was when….

From this failure, I learned….

Now, use the STAR technique to package your answer. Practice it to keep it under two minutes. And don't forget your follow-up, "Did that answer your question?"

Remember, you get to choose which failure you share. It doesn't have to be what you consider to be your biggest failure. It just has to be a real failure, not an humble brag that actually shows a strength instead of a failure.

I failed to realize that operations management would drain the life out of me. I had a very low tolerance for dealing with the exact same dysfunctional behaviors every month, especially when I knew that the parties had been properly trained in their work and understood the importance of doing their work in a quality and timely manner. My impatience led to minor issues turning into noise (emails flying back and forth, hither and yon) which turned on me, to distract from the dysfunctional behavior of the offender.

I failed to realize that I was walking into a very confrontational situation and I took no precautions to provide a way to de-escalate without abject capitulation (which would have made it impossible for me to continue working as an effective project manager).

These are real failures and real lessons from my life.

When you respond with honest answers, in a concise manner and you don't wait for them to ask what you learned from the experience, you demonstrate several desirable qualities:

1. Self-awareness. You understand your limitations.

2. Honesty. You gave a real answer.

3. The ability to learn and grow.

4. The ability to persist in the face of adversity.

Who doesn't want to hire all that?

9 HANDLING SILLY INTERVIEW QUESTIONS

Silly, touchy-feely interview questions are a pet peeve of mine. Some interviewers mistakenly think that these questions provide some kind of insight into the personality of the job seeker. At best, all they really do is allow the candidate to demonstrate how they can game the system with a glib answer and handle an inane interviewer.

Some people believe that there is some actual psychological foundations beneath these questions. One recent article called, "The 100 Most Ridiculous Job Interview Questions Ever" [1] asserted that "These questions may sound daft, but they are aimed at learning something about how you see yourself."

The unfortunate truth is that these interview questions have no actual basis in psychology as it relates to job performance.

If an interviewer wants to find out your attitudes or aptitudes, there are valid behavioral interviewing techniques that can be used to do this. However, they require both training and serious effort on the part of the interviewer and most interviewers have only gotten on-the-job training.

Since the purpose of this book is to teach you how to be interviewed, rather than how to conduct an interview I won't say any more on this topic except this. For an interviewer to build valid behavioral interview questions, they have to consciously identify the traits that they are looking for in the candidate and then construct a question that will allow the job seeker to explain an actual experience in their life that will demonstrate either the presence or absence of the desired trait. Using inane, off-the-wall questions to reveal actual personality traits is like trying to tune a violin with your hands encased in cement blocks. You will get the violin to make some noise, but it won't be pretty and you will likely trash the violin.

The most inane question I heard in an interview recently was offered by a colleague of mine. He asked, "which of the Star Trek Captains would you be?"

Other silly questions I have heard over the years are:

- "If you were an animal, what kind of animal would you be?" and,
- "If you were a food, what food would you be?"

From the article I mentioned above, here are a few more silly questions.

1. If you could be Batman or Robin, which one would you be?
2. What football team do you Support? – Why them?
3. Do you prefer cats or dogs?
4. Sing a song that best describes you.
5. If aliens landed in front of you and, in exchange for anything you desire, offered you any position on their planet, what would you want?
6. If Hollywood made a movie about your life, whom would you like to see play the lead role as you?
7. What would I find in your fridge right now?
8. How would you design a spice rack for a blind person?
9. If you were a character from Star Wars, which one would you be?

10. If you were shrunk to the size of a pencil and put in a blender, how would you get out?

11. If you were a salad, what kind of dressing would you have?

12. If you were a bicycle, what part would you be?

13. What is your favorite flavor of ice cream?

14. Why do you think Charles Chaplin is famous?

15. Which ancient place would you like to go?

16. What will you do if you have a time machine?

17. What would you like to ask from the God?

18. How would you react if you are transformed into a fish?

19. If you are a god what would you do to the world?

20. You are hosting a dinner party and must invite 3 famous people. Who would you choose and why?

Twenty of these are enough for me.

If you get asked any of these idiotic questions, I hope you will maintain your composure, regardless of the temptation to dismiss the interviewer as an idiot and walk out.

When I was active in Toastmasters I learned a valuable technique for public speaking which applies here.

During a regular exercise called "Table Topics" each member is presented with a question (which may be random) and asked to speak on it for at least two minutes.

Given the often random nature of the questions it was common to get a question which either was about something I knew nothing about, or was one where I knew that my heartfelt answer would be very politically incorrect. Since this Toastmasters chapter was sponsored by my employer and all the members were fellow employees, any rash comment could come back to haunt me in the workplace.

An experienced Toastmaster explained what to do when presented with a question you don't want to answer. He said simply, "answer a question you do want to answer."

The technique to do this is simple.

First, repeat the question, for instance, "What kind of fruit would I be?" and add, "That is a very interesting question." Think for a moment about what the interviewer is hoping you will reveal about yourself.

Then nod and respond, "I really can't say what kind of fruit I would be. But, I can tell you about a time in my experience where…" and then relate an experience from your résumé that you hope will reveal the aptitude or attitude that the interviewer is looking for.

I confess that if I were presented with more than one such question, I would probably end the interview myself. In my opinion, it would indicate one of two possibilities, neither of which are very encouraging.

1.   The interviewer has decided not to hire you and s/he is just killing time and prodding to see what kind of answer you will give to a silly question.

2.   The interviewer is a total idiot and not the sort of person you want to have as a coworker, or worse, as a boss.

In either of these cases, it is best to disengage from the interview in a polite manner, even if you must pretend that you just received an urgent text that someone close to you was just in a wreck and you need to go to the hospital.

10 A FEW WORDS ABOUT YOUR RÉSUMÉ

I know it may seem odd for me to bring up your résumé in a book about tips for effective interviews. Trust me on this, your résumé is an indispensible part of an effective interview.

Today, I looked at a résumé that a recruiter had submitted for a job opening. After reading it, I refused to give the candidate an interview. The candidate was clearly not a fit for the role and I wasn't willing to waste my time and energy interviewing someone who I definitely was not going to hire.

A couple of days ago this same recruiter noticed that a lot of his candidates were getting rejected without even getting an interview. He reached out to my colleague and I expressing his concern that he wasn't meeting our needs.

Here is a portion of what I told him that he and his compadres needed to do differently if they wanted to have an higher success rate with the people they are trying to get hired.

If you are a recruiter, consider what I say below. If you are a job seeker, pay attention and do what you can to fix this situation on your own. And, while some of this is specific to project management roles, consider your own field of expertise and apply these lessons to your resume.

-------- (originally published on my blog 3/4/16)

Regarding several recent candidates from your company and others, here is what I have seen.

Candidates whose experience is legitimate, but not sufficient for this role (this is a Sr Enterprise Project Management role).

- They typically have not managed projects with enterprise-wide impacts
- They typically have not managed projects with $10mm budgets or larger
- They are a tier 1 (Jr/entry level), tier 2 pm, or tier 3 (Sr PM), and lack the experience that a Senior Enterprise PM typically brings to the table.

This is where cold hard numbers are your first ally.

Candidates whose Project Management experience is manufactured (aka "resume inflation")

Their résumé summary mentions project management as a skill – BUT

- Their résumé does not reflect any position where they held the title of project manager
- Their résumé experience does not reflect experiences where they had to display key PM skills such as project planning, risk management, issue escalation, stakeholder management, etc.

- Often these latter are people who have held roles as Business or Systems Analysts or Project Leads. Those roles may give them some PM skills, but it is not the same as actually having the PM role.
- Many of these are people who were asked to act as the PM while also working as an individual contributor in the project. Experience has shown that people in this situation are exposed to PM deliverables and skills, but have not had the opportunity to develop those skills to the level required to manage a project of the size and complexity that we are handling here at our project. They are an entry level PM, at best.

If your résumé doesn't reflect the experience required for a position, the odds are that you won't get an interview.

If you are seeking positions in different fields, create a specific résumé for each field. The résumé should reflect relevant experience.

If you don't have the experience at the level needed for the role, getting the job will be your worst nightmare, followed by the humiliation of getting demoted or fired.

Résumés which reflect PM skills as "responsibilities", but do not contain any "accomplishments."

When you list responsibilities for a position you held, all that says is that your employer expected you to deliver this, not that you actually did any of that.

In contrast, when you list accomplishments (especially with cold, hard numbers), you tell your prospective employer that you deliver results.

Resumes that use hyperbole

Dictionary.com defines hyperbole as obvious and intentional exaggeration.

- "Excellent" skills – excellent compared to what – a shoe shine boy?
- "razor sharp focus" – is anyone going to say they are unfocused?
- "skillfully apply" – would any candidate note a skill in their

resume that they applied clumsily?

- "highly effective" – how high is highly effective? Did it have an ROI of 500% or 5%?

I suggest you purge your candidates' resumes of these kind of adjectives. *They convey ego, not facts.*

Resumes that lack facts

I suggest that you get your candidates to put cold, hard numbers into their resumes wherever possible.

Instead of saying, "large, complex multi-million dollar projects" provide some numbers. For example, "Project Manager for Project X, consisting of a team of 14 top-level executives from across the enterprise, bringing approximately 300 team members from their organizations to work full-time and part-time on this project. Budget of $45mm with projected (or realized) $300mm profit lift to corporation."

That is the end of what I wrote to these recruiters. I hope you can see in what I told them some lessons for you. Just in case, you tuned out the relevant information about you which I gave to recruiters, in the next chapter I have provided some real-life résumé horror stories that served as the basis for my advice to recruiters.

You may find this next chapter easier to relate to.

11 REAL LIFE RÉSUMÉ HORROR STORIES
(originally published on my blog 03/12/16 www.ResumesByTom.com)

I have recently had the 'pleasure' of interviewing candidates for positions as project managers on the same contract I am currently working. My recent experience demonstrates that in spite of my books and others out there, people continue to mess up their chances for a job by either doing the wrong things or doing the right things the wrong way.

I am going to share some real-life, current examples of resume mistakes that prevent job seekers from getting an interview and then some interviewing problems that keep them from getting a job offer.

Of course, I have changed the names to protect the guilty.

Ms. Mia (or should I say, MIA?) – her most recent experience was left off of the resume. Since her résumé was redone on the recruiting company letterhead, I can't say whose fault this was, but it didn't help her case.

When we asked, are you still with Company XYZ? She had to say, "No. I have been at ABC since 2014." My reaction was, "Oh! Well then, tell me about what you are doing for them?"

The bad news about that is that with very limited time for an interview, we chewed up valuable talk-time which could have been avoided if I had seen the position in the résumé. Then, I could have asked specifically about anything in that experience that seemed relevant.

Unfortunately for Ms. Mia, having the up-to-date résumé wouldn't have made a difference, because Ms. Mia had interviewing skill issues that kept me from moving her to the next round of interviews.

Her résumé had indicators that she might be qualified for the role, which is why she got the initial interview.

Her problem was that during the interview she failed to articulate her answers in ways and words that made it clear that she had actually worked in the same kind of role I was looking to fill. This left me uneasy and without a clear understanding of her skill set.

Mr. Nickels – After looking at his résumé, I wouldn't consider him for this role. He was a nickel and we needed a dollar.

He had PM experience but not at the right level. His budgets were $1.5mm to $2mm. This is not comparable to the $10mm+ level of experience/impact/seasoning that is needed for a PM in where I am working right now.

In this case, Mr. Nickels didn't do anything wrong. His résumé gave me the numbers I needed to know that he would not be a good fit. I know from situations where it has occurred that hiring a person into a role that is too far above their skill set level is bad for everyone.

I remember the first time I experienced the reality of this.

In spite of my reservations (which was really just a gut feel which I couldn't clearly articulate), my teammates decided to hire a new team member. Within weeks (literally less than a month) she began to fail because her skills were a match in type, but not in level for the job.

She protested that she could bring in her deliverables in three months, not the three weeks the timeline called for. All the rest of the team members could meet those deliverables in that schedule, because their game was that much better (higher level) than hers.

We had to manage her out, which is a painful HR nightmare for everyone involved. It is not an experience I am eager to repeat and it is not any fun for anyone involved. It is especially painful for the person being managed out.

The woman in question suffered financially and emotionally from the process and our team suffered from the lost productivity and missed client expectations from her sub-level performance.

So, I learned how to match both skill set and level of skill to positions. I also learned how to discern it in résumés and uncover it in interviews.

Mr. Fantastic – I might have interviewed him based on his résumé. But if his "multi-million dollar … complex healthcare systems" project listed in his most recent experience turned out to have a budget of less than $10mm, I would have wanted to end the interview right then.

But, what really kept me from wanting to interview him was his liberal use of hyperbole in his resume.

He had "Excellent" skills – excellent compared to what – a shoe shine boy?

He had a "razor sharp focus." Is anyone going to confess to being unfocused in a resume?

He would "skillfully apply" – would any candidate note a skill in their resume that they applied clumsily?

He was "highly effective." How high is up? How much better is someone who is highly effective versus someone who is just effective?

Is highly effective delivering an ROI of 500% or 5%? I guess that depends on if the project cost was $5 or $50 million.   A 500% ROI on a $5 investment means you turned $5 into $25. And although 5% on $50 million means $2.5 million, it also means that the payback period is 10 years.

I suggest you purge your resume of these kind of adjectives and adverbs. They convey ego, not facts.

Yes, this is pretty much exactly what I told the recruiters to do too. I repeated some and expanded it here in case you missed the points I was making that apply to you as a job seeker.

Ms. Madeup - Ms. Madeup is not a specific person, rather she appears in many résumés in the form of something referred to as "résumé inflation." Résumé inflation most commonly occurs in two ways:

       1) Your résumé summary or skills list mentions a skill set, but your résumé experience (and maybe your actual experience) does not reflect any role where you actually had to work in roles that required that as a primary skill set.

I covered this same info in the previous chapter, so if you want to review it go back and read it there.

       2) Your resume lists skills as "responsibilities", but doesn't contain any "accomplishments" that reflect those skills. Providing a list of responsibilities without accomplishments that relate to those responsibilities may be read as you were responsible for a lot of things, but didn't do them, and that is why you are now looking for a new job.

Résumés that lack facts

Although I covered this in the prior chapter, this is from a slightly different perspective which I believe will be worth you taking the time to read.

Résumés that are laced with "excellent skills" often lack cold, hard facts. Facts and numbers tend to tell their own story and often your willingness to put out your numbers for all the world to see suggests a level of confidence and self-awareness that is too frequently missing in job applicants.

I suggest that you put cold, hard numbers into your résumé wherever possible.

Instead of saying, "large, complex multi-million dollar projects" provide some numbers. For example, "Project Manager for Project X, consisting of a team of 14 top-level executives from across the enterprise, bringing approximately 300 team members from their organizations to work full-time and part-time on this project. Budget of $15mm with projected (or realized) $300mm profit lift to corporation."

And When You Get an Interview

Okay, if you managed to avoid those résumé pitfalls and you actually got an appointment for an interview, now, you need to do a few things to nail it in the interview.

When you are asked a question in the interview make sure you answer it in less than five minutes. If you cannot give a clear and concise answer in five minutes, then you haven't practiced your answers. If you don't think you can practice your answers, then you haven't given enough thought to what you have actually done in your career.

If you are unable to quickly and clearly cite specific experiences that answer interview questions your actual experience will remain unknown and you are unlikely to progress to an offer.

Consider your answers carefully and **listen** to the questions you are asked.

Even **when asked a hypothetical question** (e.g., "how would you …?"), instead of saying what you would do, you should respond by pointing to a specific instance in your experience where you handled this kind of situation. You should explain the situation, what you did, and what resulted from your actions.

Even for interviewers who habitually ask these (in my opinion worthless) hypothetical questions, answers that highlight actual experience over theory are more impactful.

Hypothetical questions and hypothetical answers are, in my view, only useful when interviewing an entry-level candidate.

Unfortunately, many interviewers have never received good training in how to interview in ways that allows them to uncover the relevant experience a candidate has to offer, so these hypothetical questions are very common.

When a candidate tells me what they "would do" or "typically do" (the latter is slightly better), they are talking theory rather than experience. They might be using Google while on the phone to scan the highpoints from an online article to answer the question, or they may be relying on what they learned in a class. In either of those instances, they are talking theory because they have never actually done it. When the candidate says what they "typically do", that is a stronger response, but it still lacks the validation that comes from telling about a relevant experience and what they actually did do.

Avoid using "we-speak".

You should be very clear to delineate what the team ("we") was asked to do, and what you ("I") did. I know that we are all indoctrinated in team mentality and not hogging glory, but you are being hired, not the team.

Personally, when a candidate consistently says "we", and fails to tell me what "I" did, I read that (right or wrong) as someone who is trying to benefit from what others on the team did, regardless of how little the individual actually contributed to the success of the endeavor. We need individuals who can pull their own weight, not people who rely on others in the team to make up for their weaknesses.

12 A FUNNY THING HAPPENED ON THE WAY TO THE INTERVIEW

(originally published on my blog 3/2/16 www.ResumesByTom.com)

Many years ago, for the first time, I watched Zero Mostel perform "A Funny Thing Happened On The Way To The Forum", a farcical comedy that borders on slapstick in places. I laughed then, and I laugh now when I see it as a play or a movie. The story is full of funny, unexpected and unbelievable twists.

Much like in the play, I had something funny and unexpected happen to me the other day when I was interviewing a job candidate - he quoted me to me.

An associate and I were doing a phone interview for a project manager position. When I introduced myself, the candidate said, "Tom Sheppard, the author of 'Fire Yourself: Get the Job You Want', and 'Five Ways to Blow an Interview'?"

Clearly, the candidate had done some in-depth research on who was going to interview him. I was impressed, but I didn't let it go to my head and influence the interview.

Fortunately, his research also extended to the project and he was able to give my associate an overview of our work here that was as concise and comprehensive as any I have heard her give to the many job candidates we have interviewed together. That left us both with a very positive impression.

Take note any Recruiters out there - if this guy could get a good read on our project, you should be able to as well and use it to both screen and prepare your candidates for their interview. Too many job candidates come to the initial interview with faulty or totally wrong ideas of the what the project is and the role itself. That wastes everyone's time and effort.

Then, during the interview he did a couple of things right out of my book "<u>A Job Hunter's Primer</u>." He then pointed out that he had learned them from me.

What He Did
Answering a question, he made it a point to use the 'star' technique of telling us about a situation or task (ST), the specific actions he took (A), and the results of his efforts (R). And then, he followed up by asking, "did I answer your question?"

These are both techniques I have taught many people over the years for how to nail your job interview.

I learned the STAR technique when I was trained in behavioral interviewing. I realized then that it was a valuable tool for any job seeker, because it would allow them to answer questions with facts from their backgrounds instead of giving hypothetical answers. It would allow them to give those factual answers in a way that delivered a powerful impression of a person who can think clearly and has experience to back up the claims in their resume.

Ever since then, I have been using that technique when I conduct interviews - to cut through the BS and uncover proven performance and work attributes in action. And, I have religiously taught it to my job-seeking clients (and coached them on it) to give them the best possible chance to get the offer for the job they want.

In spite of using and teaching these tools, I confess, I was a little bit discombobulated by his blatant reference to having learned this from my me. However, his application of the lesson allowed my associate and I to determine that he was sufficiently qualified for the job to move him up to the next round of interviews, which would be face-to-face.

Now, here is the rest of the story. Today, my colleague extended

CONCLUSIONS

I told you when we started this that you would see repeated themes. I know I delivered. I hope you figured out that the things I repeated are really important.

By now, you have learned how to prepare for a job interview both mentally and physically. You have learned what kind of questions to expect and how to answer them. You have learned what questions you should ask and how you can effectively control an interview while helping the person interviewing you to get what they want while you get what you want.

You have learned how to make it clear that you want the job and when you expect to hear from them about the job, so you don't have to keep waiting and waiting and waiting.

You have also learned how to use your résumé effectively during an interview to call attention to your accomplishments and to answer their questions fully and clearly.

In short, you have learned how to interview to get the job you want.

Now, go and get the job you want.

FINAL THOUGHTS

I decided to publish this book to help other people to enjoy the kind of career security I have benefitted from. I believe that if I can help other people get what they want out of life, then I will have a network of friends who will recommend and buy my books, audios, seminars or workshops. This is the law of reciprocity - give and it will be given unto you! Or as the Bible says,

"Cast your bread upon the waters and after many days it will return unto you."

I sincerely hope you have found this book helpful. And I hope you will watch for the other books in this series to help you **Get and Keep the Job You Want**.

9 798546 560416